Soul Care

GREGORY L. JANTZ, PhD
KEITH WALL

Prayers, Scriptures,
and Spiritual Practices
for When You Need
Hope the Most

TYNDALE
MOMENTUM®

The nonfiction imprint of
Tyndale House Publishers, Inc.

Visit Tyndale online at www.tyndale.com.

Visit Tyndale Momentum online at www.tyndalemomentum.com.

TYNDALE, *Tyndale Momentum*, and Tyndale's quill logo are registered trademarks of Tyndale House Publishers, Inc. The Tyndale Momentum logo is a trademark of Tyndale House Publishers, Inc. Tyndale Momentum is the nonfiction imprint of Tyndale House Publishers, Inc., Carol Stream, Illinois.

Soul Care: Prayers, Scriptures, and Spiritual Practices for When You Need Hope the Most

Designed by Jennifer Phelps

Published in association with The Bindery Agency, www.TheBinderyAgency.com.

For information about special discounts for bulk purchases, please contact Tyndale House Publishers at csresponse@tyndale.com, or call 1-800-323-9400.

ISBN 978-1-4964-3466-1

Printed in China

25	24	23	22	21	20	19
7	6	5	4	3	2	1

I pray that God, the source of hope, will fill you completely with joy and peace because you trust in him. Then you will overflow with confident hope through the power of the Holy Spirit.

ROMANS 15:13

Contents

Introduction

*Hope is called the anchor of the soul (Hebrews 6:19), because
it gives stability to the Christian life. But hope is not simply
a "wish" . . . rather, it is that which latches on to the certainty
of the promises of the future that God has made.*

R. C. SPROUL

Feeling a little anxious? Worried? Depressed? You're not
alone. In the thirty-plus years that I've been treating
depression, I can't remember a time when free-floating
anxiety and depression have been more prevalent. And
it's no wonder. Look around. It seems everywhere
we turn these days, we find uncertainty—economic
uncertainty, political uncertainty. Even churches and
other faith communities aren't immune. Every day, our
smartphones keep us tethered to a relentless barrage
of news and information coming at us faster than we
can possibly absorb it. Divisiveness has taken over the
airwaves and has turned social media into a veritable
battleground pitting brother against brother and friend
against friend. We're living in a world of extremes, and

all too often, we find ourselves trapped in the middle, feeling overwhelmed, isolated, and not sure who we can trust or who we can believe. Sometimes it feels as though all hope is lost.

The book you are holding in your hands right now, however, is your plan for hope. I call it *Soul Care* because that is exactly what it is: a plan for caring for your soul. But *Soul Care* is not simply a program to follow—it's a way of life. When practiced regularly, it can transform you from the inside out, shining light on the old things that no longer serve you and pointing to new ways of being that will.

As beloved pastor Charles Swindoll once said, "No matter how dark the clouds, the sun will eventually pierce the darkness and dispel it; no matter how heavy the rain, the sun will ultimately prevail to hang a rainbow in the sky."[1]

That's God's promise to us—and God always keeps his promises! But we have a role to play as well. Our job, quite simply, is to have faith.

Faith is not an ethereal "thing" that we simply try to grasp. It's an action verb—something we do on purpose. It takes effort and discipline. But I can assure you, the hope that's restored when you choose faith over despair is *real*. It's the priceless assurance that you are loved beyond all reason by a Creator who never takes his eyes off you.

In Jeremiah 29:11, we are told, "'I know the plans I have for you,' says the LORD. 'They are plans for good and not for disaster, to give you a future and a hope.'"

In other words, God is willing and able to meet you exactly where you are and to carry you for as long as it takes to restore your strength. But having faith is *your* role to play. Faith is like a jolt of energy that activates our spiritual and emotional immune system as nothing else can. It's what enables us to actively complete the circuit of God's love by choosing to believe we are not alone—through sheer force of will, if necessary—when the night is at its darkest. Faith is what keeps our internal compass pointed north. Faith is what makes hope possible. And as we learn in Jeremiah, true hope comes when we have a plan.

The following pages will introduce you to nine spiritual disciplines that will help you focus your heart and mind on God; let go of the bitterness, pain, guilt, fear, and anxiety that have been holding you captive; develop a solid support network; and renew your spirit one day at a time. How you use this book is up to you. My advice is to start small. Choose one discipline to begin with, and then when you're comfortable, add another. Spend time meditating on the Scripture verses. Let God speak to you through them. If you're able, commit them to memory so they'll always be top of mind when you need a quick jolt of encouragement. There is no wisdom greater than God's Word—and no promises more powerful. If you consistently work to incorporate these spiritual disciplines into your life, in time you will discover a life free from anxiety, filled with hope, and infused with the kind of beauty, joy, and meaning that only God can bring.

There will always be uncertainty and suffering in the world. But as a follower of Jesus Christ, you were not born to suffer or to barely survive. You were born to *thrive*. God wants you to experience healing in your life. He wants the sunshine to break through the dark clouds obscuring your view. He wants to send a rainbow of healing so you can experience once again the fullness and joyfulness he intended for you all along. Enjoy the journey.

Dr. Gregory Jantz

PART 1

The Spiritual Practices

PRAYER

There is not in the world a kind of life more sweet and delightful than that of a continual conversation with God.

BROTHER LAWRENCE

Perhaps the most important spiritual discipline to adopt in your daily life is prayer. Now, when I write "pray," I don't mean muttering a stream of rote, repetitious phrases you heard in church a long time ago. I'm talking about regular, honest, heartfelt conversations with the one who created you, who loves you, and who desperately wants you to know him as intimately as he knows you.

So what should you talk about? Everything! There is no problem too big or too small to go to God with for help. As Elisabeth Elliot once said, "If you believe in a God who controls the big things, you have to believe in a God who controls the little things."[2] Ask him for wisdom and guidance. Ask him to give you the courage and strength to get through the tough times. But don't stop there! Tell him about all the wonderful things that are happening in your life as well. Thank him for the daily blessings of family and friends. Share your accomplishments, your dreams, and your goals for the future. Talk to him about every aspect of your life, good and bad. It's so easy to get mired in negativity. Regularly scheduled prayer time provides a wonderful opportunity to reflect on and express gratitude for everything that is going *right* in our lives.

If you're not used to talking with God or you aren't sure how or where to start, try writing him a letter or pairing your prayer time with another activity like going for a walk. Whatever you do, don't overthink it! God isn't concerned with eloquence or fancy language. He just wants to hear from you. So be yourself. Before you know it, you'll be looking forward to your daily quiet time with God. You may even start talking with him throughout your day! Nothing soothes the soul and quiets the mind like quality time spent in the company of a dear and trusted friend. So get into the habit of giving yourself a daily dose of hope. God would love to hear from you!

Scripture to Soothe Your Soul

Don't worry about anything; instead, pray about everything. Tell God what you need, and thank him for all he has done.

PHILIPPIANS 4:6

I tell you, you can pray for anything, and if you believe that you've received it, it will be yours.

MARK 11:24

When you pray, go away by yourself, shut the door behind you, and pray to your Father in private. Then your Father, who sees everything, will reward you.

MATTHEW 6:6

Are any of you suffering hardships? You should pray. Are any of you happy? You should sing praises. Are any of you sick? You should call for the elders of the church to come and pray over you, anointing you with oil in the name of the Lord. Such a prayer offered in faith will heal the sick, and the Lord will make you well. And if you have committed any sins, you will be forgiven.

Confess your sins to each other and pray for each other so that you may be healed. The earnest prayer of a righteous person has great power and produces wonderful results. Elijah was as human as we are, and yet when he prayed earnestly that no rain would fall, none fell for three and a half years!

JAMES 5:13-17

Pray then like this:

"Our Father in heaven,
hallowed be your name.
Your kingdom come,
your will be done,
    on earth as it is in heaven.
Give us this day our daily bread,
and forgive us our debts,
    as we also have forgiven our debtors.
And lead us not into temptation,
    but deliver us from evil."

MATTHEW 6:9-13, ESV

We are confident that he hears us whenever we ask for anything that pleases him. And since we know he hears us when we make our requests, we also know that he will give us what we ask for.

1 JOHN 5:14-15

At that time you won't need to ask me for anything. I tell you the truth, you will ask the Father directly, and he will grant your request because you use my name. You haven't done this before. Ask, using my name, and you will receive, and you will have abundant joy.

JOHN 16:23-24

Morning, noon, and night
 I cry out in my distress,
 and the LORD hears my voice.

PSALM 55:17

If you remain in me [Jesus] and my words remain in you, you may ask for anything you want, and it will be granted!

JOHN 15:7

The Holy Spirit helps us in our weakness. For example, we don't know what God wants us to pray for. But the Holy Spirit prays for us with groanings that cannot be expressed in words.

ROMANS 8:26

Wisdom to Awaken Your Spirit

Our prayers may be awkward. Our attempts may be feeble. But since the power of prayer is in the one who hears it and not in the one who says it, our prayers do make a difference.

MAX LUCADO

Prayer does not mean simply to pour out one's heart. It means rather to find the way to God and to speak with him, whether the heart is full or empty.

DIETRICH BONHOEFFER

Our prayers lay the track down which God's power can come. Like a mighty locomotive, his power is irresistible, but it cannot reach us without rails.

WATCHMAN NEE

There are parts of our calling, works of the Holy Spirit, and defeats of the darkness that will come no other way than furious, fervent, faith-filled, unceasing prayer.

BETH MOORE

You can do more than pray after you have prayed; but you can never do more than pray until you have prayed.

A. J. GORDON

The reality is, my prayers don't change God. But, I am convinced prayer changes me. Praying boldly boots me out of that stale place of religious habit into authentic connection with God Himself.

LYSA TERKEURST

If you believe in prayer at all, expect God to hear you. If you do not expect, you will not

have. God will not hear you unless you believe
He will hear you; but if you believe He will, He
will be as good as your faith.

CHARLES SPURGEON

Prayer does not mean that I am to bring God
down to my thoughts and my purposes, and
bend His government according to my foolish,
silly, and sometimes sinful notions. Prayer
means that I am to be raised up into feeling,
into union and design with Him; that I am
to enter into His counsel, and carry out His
purpose fully.

D. L. MOODY

It matters little what form of prayer we adopt
or how many words we use. What matters is
the faith which lays hold on God, knowing
that He knows our needs before we even
ask Him. That is what gives Christian prayer
its boundless confidence and its joyous
certainty.

DIETRICH BONHOEFFER

Prayer does not influence God. Prayer surely does influence God. It does not influence His purpose. It does influence His action.

S. D. GORDON

Prayer is the way you defeat the devil . . . reach the lost . . . restore a backslider . . . strengthen the saints . . . send missionaries out . . . cure the sick . . . [and] accomplish the impossible.

DAVID JEREMIAH

Prayer for Hope and Healing

Lord, there are so many things happening in my life right now—some good, some difficult—and sometimes I fall into the trap of feeling as though I have to face all of them by myself. What a relief it is knowing that you are always there, always listening, and always providing whatever strength and wisdom I might need. Your Scripture is a constant reminder to me that I should not "worry about anything, but rather, pray about everything." Thank you, Lord, for being a constant companion, for never tiring of my complaints or cries for help, for your patience when I struggle to say or do what is right, and for lifting me up when I am struggling to stand on my own. I treasure the time we spend together every day, Lord. Your faithful presence, thoughtful guidance, and unending love are gifts I value beyond measure. Thank you, Lord, for our time today, for all that you have already done in my life, and for all we have yet to do together.

In Jesus' name, amen.

HEARING
GOD'S VOICE

Having your spiritual radar up in constant anticipation
of His presence—even in the midst of the joyful chaos and
regular rhythms of your everyday living—is paramount
in hearing God, because sometimes the place and manner
you find Him is the least spectacular you'd expect.

PRISCILLA SHIRER

Many people scoff at the idea that God actually "speaks" to us, because they've never heard an audible voice answer them directly. But God speaks to us all the time! We just don't recognize it because our definition of "voice" is a little too narrow. But the psalmist writes,

The heavens proclaim the glory of God.
    The skies display his craftsmanship.
Day after day they continue to speak;
    night after night they make him known.
They speak without a sound or word;
    their voice is never heard.

> Yet their message has gone throughout the earth,
> and their words to all the world.

PSALM 19:1-4

As this psalm so eloquently describes, God *does* speak to us through nature—his presence can be seen and felt in every breathtaking sunrise and sunset, in the colorful hues of a rainbow after a storm, and in the awesome power of a waterfall or the crashing surf. And that's just the beginning! God's voice can also be heard in art and music and in stories that inspire us to be more and do better. He speaks in every act of kindness, no matter how small. He speaks through the love of our families and friends and the faithful companionship of our pets. He also speaks to us through our dreams and in subtle moments of intuition.

But like every conversation, it's possible not to hear a word of it. Why? Because when we get all wrapped up in our own drama, we're usually so busy talking, we forget to stop and listen! The next time you talk to God, slow down, be quiet, and extend your awareness. If you don't feel or hear anything at first, don't panic. That's perfectly normal. Just like *talking* to God, sometimes *listening* for him takes time and practice. But once you make a habit of opening yourself up to hearing his voice and feeling his presence, you'll soon discover that evidence of God's love is all around you. So take a walk in the woods, plop yourself down on a park bench, or just sit in your backyard and listen to the birds singing. Go looking for the diverse love notes from God that litter the world—and you will find them.

Scripture to Soothe Your Soul

Ask me and I [the Lord] will tell you remarkable secrets you do not know about things to come.
JEREMIAH 33:3

We are confident that he [the Son of God] hears us whenever we ask for anything that pleases him. And since we know he hears us when we make our requests, we also know that he will give us what we ask for.
1 JOHN 5:14-15

The voice of the LORD echoes above the sea.
The God of glory thunders.
The LORD thunders over the mighty sea.

The voice of the LORD is powerful;
    the voice of the LORD is majestic.
The voice of the LORD splits the mighty cedars;
    the LORD shatters the cedars of Lebanon.
He makes Lebanon's mountains skip like a calf;
    he makes Mount Hermon leap like a young
        wild ox.
The voice of the LORD strikes
    with bolts of lightning.

PSALM 29:3-7

Ever since the world was created, people have seen the earth and sky. Through everything God made, they can clearly see his invisible qualities—his eternal power and divine nature. So they have no excuse for not knowing God.

ROMANS 1:20

Faith comes from hearing, and hearing through the word of Christ.

ROMANS 10:17, ESV

When the Spirit of truth comes, he will guide you into all truth. He will not speak on his own

but will tell you what he has heard. He will tell
you about the future.

JOHN 16:13

Don't be afraid, for I [the Lord] am with you.
    Don't be discouraged, for I am your God.
I will strengthen you and help you.
    I will hold you up with my victorious right
        hand.

ISAIAH 41:10

The LORD your God is living among you.
    He is a mighty savior.
He will take delight in you with gladness.
    With his love, he will calm all your fears.
    He will rejoice over you with joyful songs.

ZEPHANIAH 3:17

Those who accept my [Jesus'] commandments
and obey them are the ones who love me. And
because they love me, my Father will love them.
And I will love them and reveal myself to each
of them.

JOHN 14:21

Wisdom to Awaken Your Spirit

When praying for the Lord's will about something questionable, don't give up if you don't receive clear leading after one prayer; just keep on praying until God makes it clear.

CURTIS HUTSON

Just as in prayer it is not we who momentarily catch His attention, but He ours, so when we fail to hear His voice, it is not because He is not speaking so much as that we are not listening. . . . We must recognize that all things are in God and that God is in all things, and we must learn to be very attentive, in order to hear God speaking in His ordinary tone without any special accent.

CHARLES H. BRENT

Our prayers run along one road and God's answers by another, and by and by they meet.

ADONIRAM JUDSON

Listening is the beginning of prayer. . . . In the silence of the heart God speaks.

MOTHER TERESA

We often miss hearing God's voice simply because we aren't paying attention.

RICK WARREN

Hearing God is not all that difficult. If we know the Lord, we have already heard His voice—after all it was the inner leading that brought us to Him in the first place. But we can hear His voice once and still miss His best if we don't keep on listening. After the *what* of guidance comes the *when* and *how*.

LOREN CUNNINGHAM

God is waiting to be found everywhere, in the darkest corners of our lives, the dead ends and bad neighborhoods we wake up in, and in the simplest, lightest, most singular and luminous moments. He's hiding, like a child, in quite obvious and visible places, because he wants to be found. The miracle is that he dwells in both.

SHAUNA NIEQUIST

The essence of meditation is a period of time set aside to contemplate the Lord, listen to Him, and allow Him to permeate our spirits.

CHARLES STANLEY

There's a time for everything in your life. God alone knows what that is. And because His Spirit dwells within you, and because He is deeply interested in helping you experience the fullness of His plans for your life, you can just stay tuned and know that He'll make it clear to you right on time, even as He keeps you loved and encouraged by His presence all along the way.

PRISCILLA SHIRER

God can use the words of a teenager, the prayer of a senior citizen, or the candid remark of a child to convict you of the need to make changes in your life.

HENRY T. BLACKABY

Prayer for Hope and Healing

God, nobody knows more about me than you do. You are with me wherever I go. You know my thoughts, my fears, my strengths, and my shortcomings. You know every question that I have and every concern that weighs on my heart—even before I come to you with them. Help me to know you as well as you know me. Help me to feel your presence not just in times of worship or prayer but everywhere I go and in everything I do. Lord, help me to tune out the distractions that threaten to drown out your voice so that I can draw closer to you. Teach me to hear your voice in the melody of birds singing, to see your face in the innocent smiles of children at play, and to feel your love in the heartfelt companionship of family and friends.

In your Son's name, amen.

GRATITUDE

*Gratitude produces deep, abiding joy because we know
that God is working in us, even through difficulties.*

CHARLES STANLEY

Why should we make a habit of regularly experiencing and expressing gratitude? Because simply put, gratitude fosters optimism, and optimism fuels hope. And hope is what gives us the strength to keep moving forward on even our darkest days. That's why it's hard to imagine more effective soul medicine than gratitude—it's impossible to feel grateful and hopeless at the same time!

Granted, sometimes when we're really struggling, gratitude can be hard to muster. So start with the small things. Anyone can come up with those—and the more whimsical, the better. For example, I'm grateful for ice cream and for the inspired genius who invented it. I'm grateful that freshly mown grass is part of my world on summer evenings. I'm grateful for how it smells and how it feels on bare feet. I'm even grateful for rainy days, because I love the way the air smells after a storm passes. As you have your daily conversations with God, make a habit of thanking him for something that brings you joy.

The medieval Christian philosopher and mystic Meister Eckhart once said, "If the only prayer you ever say in your entire life is thank you, it will be enough." And if you think about it, the list of things we can and should be thankful for—even in our darkest moments—is practically inexhaustible. So say thank you—out loud and with gusto—for teriyaki sauce or butterflies or kites or Mozart . . . anything that has ever made you smile. Say thank you for hot showers and soft towels. For roller coasters and baseball. Say thank you for Elvis Presley and fireworks. For tulips poking out of the dirt in the spring and that magic moment when the lights go down in the movie theater.

The wonderful thing about gratitude is that it is a multiplier—not of the beauty and good all around us in the world (that never changes) but of our awareness of it and of the loving God responsible for it all. When dark thoughts threaten to push everything else aside, practicing purposeful gratitude to our Creator is a powerful way to push back.

Scripture to Soothe Your Soul

Give thanks for everything to God the Father in the name of our Lord Jesus Christ.

EPHESIANS 5:20

Let the peace that comes from Christ rule in your hearts. For as members of one body you are called to live in peace. And always be thankful. Let the message about Christ, in all its richness, fill your lives. Teach and counsel each other with all the wisdom he gives. Sing psalms and hymns and spiritual songs to God with thankful hearts. And whatever you do or say, do it as a representative of the Lord Jesus, giving thanks through him to God the Father.

COLOSSIANS 3:15-17

Shout with joy to the LORD, all the earth!
    Worship the LORD with gladness.
    Come before him, singing with joy.
Acknowledge that the LORD is God!
    He made us, and we are his.
    We are his people, the sheep of his pasture.
Enter his gates with thanksgiving;
    go into his courts with praise.
    Give thanks to him and praise his name.
For the LORD is good.
    His unfailing love continues forever,
    and his faithfulness continues to each
        generation.

PSALM 100:1-5

You are my God, and I will praise you!
    You are my God, and I will exalt you!

Give thanks to the LORD, for he is good!
    His faithful love endures forever.

PSALM 118:28-29

Not that I was ever in need, for I have learned
how to be content with whatever I have.

I know how to live on almost nothing or with everything. I have learned the secret of living in every situation, whether it is with a full stomach or empty, with plenty or little. For I can do everything through Christ, who gives me strength.

PHILIPPIANS 4:11-13

As Jesus continued on toward Jerusalem, he reached the border between Galilee and Samaria. As he entered a village there, ten men with leprosy stood at a distance, crying out, "Jesus, Master, have mercy on us!"

He looked at them and said, "Go show yourselves to the priests." And as they went, they were cleansed of their leprosy.

One of them, when he saw that he was healed, came back to Jesus, shouting, "Praise God!" He fell to the ground at Jesus' feet, thanking him for what he had done. This man was a Samaritan.

Jesus asked, "Didn't I heal ten men? Where are the other nine? Has no one returned to give glory to God except this foreigner?" And Jesus said to the man, "Stand up and go. Your faith has healed you."

LUKE 17:11-19

The faithful love of the LORD never ends!
    His mercies never cease.
Great is his faithfulness;
    his mercies begin afresh each morning.
I say to myself, "The LORD is my inheritance;
    therefore, I will hope in him!"

LAMENTATIONS 3:22-24

Count it all joy, my brothers, when you meet trials of various kinds, for you know that the testing of your faith produces steadfastness. And let steadfastness have its full effect, that you may be perfect and complete, lacking in nothing.

JAMES 1:2-4, ESV

Now, just as you accepted Christ Jesus as your Lord, you must continue to follow him. Let your roots grow down into him, and let your lives be built on him. Then your faith will grow strong in the truth you were taught, and you will overflow with thankfulness.

COLOSSIANS 2:6-7

Don't worry about anything; instead, pray about everything. Tell God what you need, and thank him for all he has done. Then you will experience God's peace, which exceeds anything we can understand. His peace will guard your hearts and minds as you live in Christ Jesus.

PHILIPPIANS 4:6-7

Wisdom to Awaken Your Spirit

God has promised to supply all our needs. What we don't have now, we don't need now.

ELISABETH ELLIOT

God says to give thanks in everything. That doesn't mean you need to give thanks FOR everything. You don't need to give thanks FOR that bad day. Or FOR that bad relationship. Or being passed over at work. Financial hardship.

Whatever it is—you are not to give thanks FOR the difficulties, but rather IN the difficulties. That is a very important distinction, and one I think we often miss. Giving thanks IN everything shows a heart of faith that God is bigger than the difficulties and that He can use them, if you approach Him with the right heart and spirit, for your good and His glory.

TONY EVANS

It is not how much we have, but how much we enjoy, that makes happiness.

CHARLES SPURGEON

No matter what our circumstances, we can find a reason to be thankful.

DAVID JEREMIAH

In happy moments, PRAISE GOD. In difficult moments, SEEK GOD. In quiet moments, WORSHIP GOD. In painful moments, TRUST GOD. Every moment, THANK GOD.

RICK WARREN

A spirit of thanksgiving is one of the most distinctive marks of a Christian whose heart is attuned to the Lord. . . . Thank God in the midst of trials and every persecution.

BILLY GRAHAM

If there was ever a secret for unleashing God's powerful peace in a situation, it's developing a heart of true thanksgiving.

LYSA TERKEURST

The test of all happiness is gratitude; and I felt grateful. . . . Children are grateful when Santa Claus puts in their stockings gifts of toys or sweets. Could I not be grateful to Santa Claus when he put in my stockings the gift of two miraculous legs? We thank people for birthday presents of cigars and slippers. Can I thank no one for the birthday present of birth?

G. K. CHESTERTON

When I give thanks for the seemingly microscopic, I make a place for God to grow within me.

ANN VOSKAMP

No matter what you're going through . . .
backtrack and remember all the places where
God has been so faithful before in your life. And
know. Know with assurance. And boldness. And
confidence. He is the same faithful God.

LYSA TERKEURST

Prayer for Hope and Healing

Dear God, it is so easy to forget all the blessings you have
bestowed upon me—especially when life becomes overwhelming. But, Lord, please know that I am truly grateful,
not just for the material blessings you have given me—a
home, food, and clothing—but for the love and support
of family and friends, the fellowship of other believers, the
opportunity to share your Word with others, and most
important, your friendship, protection, guidance, wisdom,
and love. I am so incredibly grateful for your presence in
my life, Lord. When frustration and discouragement begin
to take hold and I am tempted to complain about all the
things I do not have, please help me to remember just how
blessed I really am, and open my eyes to opportunities to
share my many blessings with others.

In your name, amen.

CONFESSION

To confess your sins to God is not to tell him anything he doesn't already know. Until you confess them, however, they are the abyss between you. When you confess them, they become the bridge.

FREDERICK BUECHNER

We've all thought or said or done things we're not particularly proud of, and as tempting as it is to keep those less-than-perfect moments to ourselves, trying to keep a secret from our spouse, colleague, boss, or friend can be exhausting—like walking around with our pockets full of rocks. The shame, the guilt, and worst of all, the fear of being found out. After a while, it can become downright crippling—almost like an addiction. Not only the secrets, but the lies we tell ourselves and others to cover them up, are like toxins, slowly poisoning our blood until we begin to wither from the inside out.

That's where confession comes in. Confession is like emotional and spiritual detox, cleansing our souls from all the guilt, shame, and fear that's been weighing us down. It might be a little rough going through it, but finally coming clean with whatever it is we've been expending so much mental energy in hiding can be extremely liberating. That's part of what the discipline of confession is about—setting us free from the dread of discovery when we're in the wrong.

Taking responsibility for our actions is also a powerful reminder that we're only human, and that is paradoxically empowering. Fear of exposure arises, in part, from the misguided belief that we ought to be more than we are, when the fact is God expects no such thing. The moment we admit our frailties and cut ourselves some slack for them, we find the strength and the motivation to be and do better in the future.

So why not start now? It only takes a moment to confess—*I dropped the ball on that account. I lied about being sick so I could get out of going to dinner with your parents. I'm the one who put the dent in the car*—but the emotional and spiritual freedom that follows is long lasting. Yes, there may be consequences.

Feelings might be hurt. Relationships might be strained. But the sheer sense of relief that comes from confessing our mistakes or wrongdoings is like an elixir for the soul.

Scripture to Soothe Your Soul

Confess your sins to each other and pray for each other so that you may be healed. The earnest prayer of a righteous person has great power and produces wonderful results.

JAMES 5:16

Blessed is the one whose transgression is forgiven,
   whose sin is covered.
Blessed is the man against whom the LORD counts
      no iniquity,
   and in whose spirit there is no deceit.

For when I kept silent, my bones wasted away
   through my groaning all day long.
For day and night your hand was heavy upon me;
   my strength was dried up as by the heat of
      summer.

I acknowledged my sin to you,
    and I did not cover my iniquity;
I said, "I will confess my transgressions to the
        LORD,"
    and you forgave the iniquity of my sin.

PSALM 32:1-5, ESV

People who conceal their sins will not prosper,
    but if they confess and turn from them, they
        will receive mercy.

PROVERBS 28:13

Humble yourselves under the mighty power of
God, and at the right time he will lift you up in
honor.

1 PETER 5:6

If we claim we have no sin, we are only fooling
ourselves and not living in the truth. But if we
confess our sins to him, he is faithful and just
to forgive us our sins and to cleanse us from all
wickedness.

1 JOHN 1:8-9

If my [God's] people who are called by my
name will humble themselves and pray and seek
my face and turn from their wicked ways, I will
hear from heaven and will forgive their sins and
restore their land.

2 CHRONICLES 7:14

God saved you by his grace when you believed.
And you can't take credit for this; it is a gift
from God. Salvation is not a reward for the
good things we have done, so none of us can
boast about it.

EPHESIANS 2:8-9

Blessed are the poor in spirit, for theirs is the
kingdom of heaven.

Blessed are those who mourn, for they shall
be comforted.

Blessed are the meek, for they shall inherit
the earth.

Blessed are those who hunger and thirst for
righteousness, for they shall be satisfied.

MATTHEW 5:3-6, ESV

Wisdom to Awaken Your Spirit

Few things accelerate the peace process as much as humbly admitting our own wrongdoing and asking forgiveness.

LEE STROBEL

When things fall apart, the broken pieces allow all sorts of things to enter, and one of them is the presence of God.

SHAUNA NIEQUIST

God doesn't want to number your failures or count your accomplishments as much as He wants you to have an encounter with Him.

ANN VOSKAMP

There is something you can't fix, can't heal, or can't escape, and all you can do is trust God. Finding ultimate refuge in God means you become so immersed in his presence, so convinced of his goodness, so devoted to his lordship that you find even the cave is a perfectly safe place to be because he is there with you.

JOHN ORTBERG

What you and I might rate as an absolute disaster, God may rate as a pimple-level problem that will pass. He views your life the way you view a movie after you've read the book. When something bad happens, you feel the air sucked out of the theater. Everyone else gasps at the crisis on the screen. Not you. Why? You've read the book. You know how the good guy gets out of the tight spot. God views your life with the same confidence. He's not only read your story . . . he wrote it.

MAX LUCADO

If you are ready to partake of grace, you have not to atone for your sin—you have merely to accept of the atonement. All that you want to do is to cry, "God have mercy upon me," and you will receive the blessing.

DWIGHT L. MOODY

Here's the deal, y'all. God. Already. Knows. His people are a hot, sinful mess, so when we simply acknowledge that and repent, He's waiting with open arms. We don't have to justify ourselves because Jesus already did that on the cross. So the risk of repentance doesn't lead to punishment—it leads to the unilateral forgiveness and unconditional affection of our Creator Redeemer. Vegas only wished it had a payout that humongous.

LISA HARPER

Prayer for Hope and Healing

Father God, it is so easy to point out the faults and failings of others—particularly those who have hurt me in some way. So why is it always so difficult to come to you with my own shortcomings? I know you already know the deepest, darkest secrets of my heart. More important, I know that your grace and forgiveness are without limit. You have sacrificed so much for me, Lord, and given me so much. I want so desperately to please you, but sometimes my own selfish pride gets in the way of admitting my own mistakes. Please, God, grant me the courage and humility to apologize to those I have wronged, and help me to remember that there is nothing I can or should ever feel the need to hide from you. Lord, I ask that you forgive all of my sins and wrongdoings and help me keep my heart and mind focused on you.

In Jesus' name, amen.

COMMUNITY

Christian community is the place where we keep the flame of hope alive among us and take it seriously so that it can grow and become stronger in us.

HENRI NOUWEN

When life becomes overwhelming and we're struggling emotionally, it's tempting to shut down, peel off, and spend time by ourselves. But isolating ourselves from others is one of the worst things we can do. Why? Because when we're alone, we tend to wallow in our thoughts, and our minds become echo chambers, endlessly reinforcing our sense of hopelessness and despair. With no one else to help us break the cycle or shift our focus away from our problems, things can go from bad to worse in the blink of an eye.

Luckily, God never intended for us to go through life by ourselves ("It is not good for the man to be alone"—Genesis 2:18.). That's why he filled the world with other people. We are by nature relational beings, created to need both God and each other. Take one or the other away, and everything starts to unravel.

Granted, pulling yourself out of bed, getting dressed, leaving the house, and seeking out other people when you'd rather be alone may seem counterintuitive, but getting involved with a community—especially a faith-based community—can work wonders on a troubled soul! Just being around other people of faith and spending time together worshiping and studying God's Word will help take your mind off your problems and buoy your spirit. In addition, since most Christians come to their faith via one difficult road or another, odds are, you'll encounter someone who has faced the same challenges you have and can provide a nonjudgmental shoulder to lean on. Finally, being part of a community is a tangible reminder that you are not the only person who is struggling in the world. There's something very healing about being reminded that life does not revolve around you, and that even in your darkest moments, you are never uniquely alone.

If you're not already part of a church community,

find one. Or consider joining a small group or Bible study. Whatever you do, don't underestimate the power of community to help mend a troubled soul.

Scripture to Soothe Your Soul

Let us think of ways to motivate one another to acts of love and good works. And let us not neglect our meeting together, as some people do, but encourage one another.

HEBREWS 10:24-25

Two people are better off than one, for they can help each other succeed. If one person falls, the other can reach out and help. But someone who falls alone is in real trouble. Likewise, two people lying close together can keep each other warm. But how can one be warm alone? A person standing alone can be attacked and defeated, but two can stand back-to-back and conquer. Three are even better, for a triple-braided cord is not easily broken.

ECCLESIASTES 4:9-12

Where two or three gather together as my
followers, I [Jesus] am there among them.
MATTHEW 18:20

This makes for harmony among the members,
so that all the members care for each other. If
one part suffers, all the parts suffer with it, and
if one part is honored, all the parts are glad.

All of you together are Christ's body, and
each of you is a part of it.
1 CORINTHIANS 12:25-27

Don't be selfish; don't try to impress others.
Be humble, thinking of others as better than
yourselves. Don't look out only for your own
interests, but take an interest in others, too.
PHILIPPIANS 2:3-4

This is my [Jesus'] commandment: Love each
other in the same way I have loved you. There
is no greater love than to lay down one's life for
one's friends.
JOHN 15:12-13

The human body has many parts, but the many parts make up one whole body. So it is with the body of Christ. Some of us are Jews, some are Gentiles, some are slaves, and some are free. But we have all been baptized into one body by one Spirit, and we all share the same Spirit.

Yes, the body has many different parts, not just one part. If the foot says, "I am not a part of the body because I am not a hand," that does not make it any less a part of the body. And if the ear says, "I am not part of the body because I am not an eye," would that make it any less a part of the body? If the whole body were an eye, how would you hear? Or if your whole body were an ear, how would you smell anything?

But our bodies have many parts, and God has put each part just where he wants it.

1 CORINTHIANS 12:12-18

Share each other's burdens, and in this way obey the law of Christ.

GALATIANS 6:2

Most important of all, continue to show deep love for each other, for love covers a multitude of sins. Cheerfully share your home with those who need a meal or a place to stay. God has given each of you a gift from his great variety of spiritual gifts. Use them well to serve one another. Do you have the gift of speaking? Then speak as though God himself were speaking through you. Do you have the gift of helping others? Do it with all the strength and energy that God supplies. Then everything you do will bring glory to God through Jesus Christ.

1 PETER 4:8-11

Always be humble and gentle. Be patient with each other, making allowance for each other's faults because of your love. Make every effort to keep yourselves united in the Spirit, binding yourselves together with peace. For there is one body and one Spirit, just as you have been called to one glorious hope for the future. There is one Lord, one faith, one baptism, one God and Father of all, who is over all, in all, and living through all.

EPHESIANS 4:2-6

Wisdom to Awaken Your Spirit

Some roads we travel in life can feel like the ones that might break us, but that's why God surrounds us with people who will cheer us on and wipe our tears and listen as we pour out our hearts. Because often, it's not what you say but what you do that really matters.

MELANIE SHANKLE

Some Christians try to go to heaven alone, in solitude. But believers are not compared to bears or lions or other animals that wander alone. Those who belong to Christ are sheep in this respect, that they love to get together. Sheep go in flocks, and so do God's people.

CHARLES SPURGEON

The next best thing to being wise oneself is to live in a circle of those who are.

C. S. LEWIS

I think it is interesting that God designed people to need other people. We see those

cigarette advertisements with the rugged
cowboy riding around alone on a horse, and
we think that is strength, when, really, it is like
setting your soul down on a couch and not
exercising it. The soul needs to interact with
other people to be healthy.

DONALD MILLER

We are above all things loved—that is the
good news of the gospel—and loved not just
the way we turn up on Sundays in our best
clothes and on our best behavior and with our
best feet forward, but loved as we alone know
ourselves to be, the weakest and shabbiest
of what we are along with the strongest and
gladdest. To come together as people who
believe that just maybe this gospel is actually
true should be to come together like people
who have just won the Irish Sweepstakes. It
should have us throwing our arms around each
other like people who have just discovered
that every single man and woman in those
pews is not just another familiar or unfamiliar
face but is our long-lost brother and our

long-lost sister because despite the fact that we have all walked in different gardens and knelt at different graves, we have all, humanly speaking, come from the same place and are heading out into the same blessed mystery that awaits us all. This is the joy that is so apt to be missing, and missing not just from church but from our own lives—the joy of not just managing to believe at least part of the time that it is true that life is holy, but of actually running into that holiness head-on.

FREDERICK BUECHNER

Never worry alone. When anxiety grabs my mind, it is self-perpetuating. Worrisome thoughts reproduce faster than rabbits, so one of the most powerful ways to stop the spiral of worry is simply to disclose my worry to a friend. . . . The simple act of reassurance from another human being [becomes] a tool of the Spirit to cast out fear—because peace and fear are both contagious.

JOHN ORTBERG

The load, or weight, or burden of my
neighbour's glory should be laid on my back,
a load so heavy that only humility can carry it,
and the backs of the proud will be broken. It
is a serious thing to live in a society of possible
gods and goddesses, to remember that the
dullest and most uninteresting person you can
talk to may one day be a creature which, if you
saw it now, you would be strongly tempted to
worship, or else a horror and a corruption such
as you now meet, if at all, only in a nightmare.
All day long we are, in some degree, helping
each other to one or other of these destinations.
C. S. LEWIS

Too often, people who need the cheers the most
get them the least. Every day, everyone you
know faces life with eternity on the line, and
life has a way of beating people down. Every
life needs a cheering section. Every life needs a
shoulder to lean on once in a while. Every life
needs a prayer to lift them up to God. Every life
needs a hugger to wrap some arms around them

sometimes. Every life needs to hear a voice
saying, "Don't give up."

JOHN ORTBERG

Friendship is the nearest thing we know to what
religion is. God is love. And to make religion
akin to Friendship is simply to give it the
highest expression conceivable by man.

HENRY DRUMMOND

When we honestly ask ourselves which persons
in our lives mean the most to us, we often find
that it is those who, instead of giving much
advice, solutions, or cures, have chosen rather
to share our pain and touch our wounds with
a gentle and tender hand. The friend who can
be silent with us in a moment of despair or
confusion, who can stay with us in an hour of
grief and bereavement, who can tolerate not-
knowing, not-curing, not-healing, and face
with us the reality of our powerlessness, that is
the friend who cares.

HENRI NOUWEN

Christianity is not a religion or a philosophy, but a relationship and a lifestyle. The core of that lifestyle is thinking of others, as Jesus did, instead of ourselves.

RICK WARREN

Prayer for Hope and Healing

Dear God, from the beginning you knew that it was not good for people to be alone. Thank you so much for creating such a wonderful, vibrant fellowship of believers to encourage and keep us company on the journey. It is so comforting to be surrounded by others who share the same faith, beliefs, and convictions and to know that whatever advice they offer in times of crisis will be firmly rooted in your Word. You have promised us: "Where two or three gather together as my followers, I am there among them." What a wonderful image! Let us always act, when together, as though you are sitting in our midst. Let us never speak ill of one another but be loving and encouraging. Let us always have one another's best intentions at heart, and let us push each other to be the best reflection of you we can be.

In your name we pray, amen.

SERVICE

Prayer in action is love, and love in action is service. Try to give unconditionally whatever a person needs in the moment. The point is to do something, however small, and show you care through your actions by giving your time. . . . Do not worry about why problems exist in the world—just respond to people's needs.

MOTHER TERESA

One of the fastest ways to forget your own problems is to help somebody else with theirs. There is an inherent sense of well-being and joy that comes from helping others, in part because the sheer act of helping someone less fortunate than you naturally causes you to reflect upon your own good fortune. That leads to a sense of gratitude, which in turn fuels optimism and hope. Simply put, serving others naturally makes us happier.

A 2007 report published by the Corporation for

National and Community Service called *The Health Benefits of Volunteering* states, "Volunteer activities can strengthen the social ties that protect individuals from isolation during difficult times, while the experience of helping others leads to a sense of greater self-worth and trust."[3] The benefit of service is a two-way street, making life better for you as well as for those you help. One study cited in the report even concluded that people who volunteer in service to others actually live longer than those who don't. Talk about a benefit!

So what are you waiting for? The opportunities are endless. Every city in America has homeless shelters, counseling centers for victims of domestic violence, animal rescue organizations, wounded veterans programs, hospice centers, cancer support groups, suicide prevention clinics, nursing homes filled with people in need of a friend—the list could go on for pages. All of them depend on volunteers who know what it's like to need a boost. Faith communities in particular excel at providing volunteer opportunities and steering you to one that's right for you. Give it a try. Your soul will thank you for it. Think of it this way: by getting involved in church outreach in your community or by volunteering on your own, you essentially write yourself a prescription for relief from your own troubles—free of charge!

Scripture to Soothe Your Soul

I [Paul] have been a constant example of how you can help those in need by working hard. You should remember the words of the Lord Jesus: "It is more blessed to give than to receive."

ACTS 20:35

Whatever you do or say, do it as a representative of the Lord Jesus, giving thanks through him to God the Father.

COLOSSIANS 3:17

Is there any encouragement from belonging to Christ? Any comfort from his love? Any fellowship together in the Spirit? Are your hearts tender and compassionate? Then make me [Paul] truly happy by agreeing wholeheartedly with each other, loving one

another, and working together with one mind
and purpose.

PHILIPPIANS 2:1-2

Then the King will say . . . , "Come, you who
are blessed by my Father, inherit the Kingdom
prepared for you in the creation of the world.
For I was hungry, and you fed me. I was thirsty,
and you gave me a drink. I was a stranger, and
you invited me into your home. I was naked,
and you gave me clothing. I was sick, and
you cared for me. I was in prison, and you
visited me."

Then these righteous ones will reply, "Lord,
when did we ever see you hungry and feed you?
Or thirsty and give you something to drink? Or
a stranger and show you hospitality? Or naked
and give you clothing? When did we ever see
you sick or in prison and visit you?"

And the King will say, "I tell you the truth,
when you did it to one of the least of these my
brothers and sisters, you were doing it to me!"

MATTHEW 25:34-40

God has given each of you a gift from his great variety of spiritual gifts. Use them well to serve one another.

1 PETER 4:10

The generous will prosper;
> those who refresh others will themselves be
> > refreshed.

PROVERBS 11:25

He [Jesus] sat down, called the twelve disciples over to him, and said, "Whoever wants to be first must take last place and be the servant of everyone else."

MARK 9:35

Give, and you will receive. Your gift will return to you in full—pressed down, shaken together to make room for more, running over, and poured into your lap. The amount you give will determine the amount you get back.

LUKE 6:38

Watch out! Don't do your good deeds publicly, to be admired by others, for you will lose the reward from your Father in heaven. When you give to someone in need, don't do as the hypocrites do—blowing trumpets in the synagogues and streets to call attention to their acts of charity! I [Jesus] tell you the truth, they have received all the reward they will ever get. But when you give to someone in need, don't let your left hand know what your right hand is doing. Give your gifts in private, and your Father, who sees everything, will reward you.

MATTHEW 6:1-4

Let's not get tired of doing what is good. At just the right time we will reap a harvest of blessing if we don't give up.

GALATIANS 6:9

Wisdom to Awaken Your Spirit

When service is unto people, the bones can grow weary, the frustration deep. . . . When the eyes of the heart focus on God, and the hands on always washing the feet of Jesus alone—the bones, they sing joy and the work returns to its purest state: *eucharisteo*. The work becomes worship, a liturgy of thankfulness.

ANN VOSKAMP

The true power of love is found in selfless attitudes and actions that seek the best for another person without expecting anything in return. When we act in that way, the feeling of love follows close behind.

DAVID JEREMIAH

The highest form of worship is the worship of unselfish Christian service.

BILLY GRAHAM

Don't look for big things, just do small things with great love.

MOTHER TERESA

What does love look like? It has the hands to help others. It has the feet to hasten to the poor and needy. It has eyes to see misery and want. It has the ears to hear the sighs and sorrows of men. That is what love looks like.

AUGUSTINE

The more you give, the more comes back to you, because God is the greatest giver in the universe, and He won't let you outgive Him. Go ahead and try. See what happens.

RANDY ALCORN

The most obvious lesson in Christ's teaching is that there is no happiness in having or getting anything, but only in giving.

HENRY DRUMMOND

Charity—giving to the poor—is an essential part of Christian morality. . . . I do not believe one can settle how much we ought to give. I am afraid the only safe rule is to give more than we can spare. In other words, if our expenditure on comforts, luxuries, amusements, etc., is up to the standard common among those with the same income as our own, we are probably giving away too little. If our charities do not at all pinch or hamper us, I should say they are too small. There ought to be things we should like to do and cannot do because our charitable expenditure excludes them.

C. S. LEWIS

While you're figuring out what God wants you to do next—go love everybody.

BOB GOFF

Thou shalt love thy neighbour as thyself. Neither is love content with barely working no evil to our neighbour. It continually incites us to do good: as we have time, and opportunity, to do good in every possible kind, and in every possible degree to all men.

JOHN WESLEY

Prayer for Hope and Healing

God, you sent your Son not to be a king but to be a servant, so what better way to reflect your love and grace than to serve others in your name? You have given me so many unique gifts, Lord, not for my glory but for yours. As I go through my day today, help me take the focus off myself and my own problems and open my eyes to the problems and needs of those around me. Show me how I can be of help to others, and when an opportunity presents itself, grant me the compassion and the humility to do your will without asking for or expecting anything in return.

In your Son's name I pray, amen.

FORGIVENESS

Forgiveness is the key which unlocks the door of resentment and the handcuffs of hatred. It breaks the chains of bitterness and the shackles of selfishness.

CORRIE TEN BOOM

"Love your enemies" may be one of the most difficult directives Jesus ever gave his disciples. After all, it's hard to forgive someone who has hurt you. But do you know what's even harder? Carrying around years of pent-up bitterness, pain, and resentment. Unaddressed, unreleased anger is poisonous to the body, mind, and spirit. It weakens your immune system, damages your psyche, and slowly erodes your soul. So why are we so hesitant to forgive? Because, ironically, it feels good to be mad. Anger amps up our adrenaline and energizes our emotions. What's more, it's simply easier to nurture anger than to offer forgiveness. As author Frederick Buechner says,

Of the seven deadly sins, anger is possibly the most fun. To lick your wounds, to smack your lips over grievances long past, to roll over your tongue the prospect of bitter confrontations still to come, to savor to the last toothsome morsel both the pain you are given and the pain you are giving back—in many ways it is a feast fit for a king. The chief drawback is that what you are wolfing down is yourself. The skeleton at the feast is you.[4]

As long as we hang on to feelings of outrage, injustice, and the desire for payback, we keep the offense alive and the wounds fresh. In other words, we allow our enemies to hurt us even more.

We can also be hesitant to forgive those who have hurt us because our sense of justice doesn't want us to let the person off the hook. We see forgiveness as an undeserved get-out-of-jail-free card. But forgiveness isn't about letting your enemies "off the hook." In fact, it's not intended to do anything for the person who hurt you. Forgiveness lets *ourselves* off the hook by letting go of all the toxic emotions and pain we have been carrying around. In other words, forgiveness isn't a get-out-of-jail-free card for our enemies—it's a get-out-of-jail-free card for us! When we forgive those who hurt us, we set ourselves free from all of the pain and suffering that the other person inflicted upon us. Without that freedom, we will continue to carry toxic emotions that contaminate our hearts and corrupt our thoughts.

So go ahead! Give yourself a get-out-of-jail-free card and experience the freedom that forgiveness brings!

Scripture to Soothe Your Soul

Be kind to one another, tenderhearted, forgiving one another, as God in Christ forgave you.

EPHESIANS 4:32, ESV

When you are praying, first forgive anyone you are holding a grudge against, so that your Father in heaven will forgive your sins, too.

MARK 11:25

Peter came to him and asked, "Lord, how often should I forgive someone who sins against me? Seven times?"

"No, not seven times," Jesus replied, "but seventy times seven!"

MATTHEW 18:21-22

To you who are willing to listen, I [Jesus] say, love your enemies! Do good to those who hate you.

LUKE 6:27

Hatred stirs up quarrels,
   but love makes up for all offenses.

PROVERBS 10:12

Dear friends, let us continue to love one another, for love comes from God. Anyone who loves is a child of God and knows God. But anyone who does not love does not know God, for God is love.

1 JOHN 4:7-8

Get rid of all bitterness, rage, anger, harsh words, and slander, as well as all types of evil behavior.

EPHESIANS 4:31

Love is patient and kind. Love is not jealous or boastful or proud or rude. It does not demand its own way. It is not irritable, and it keeps no record of being wronged. It does not rejoice about injustice but rejoices whenever the truth wins out. Love never gives up, never loses faith, is always hopeful, and endures through every circumstance.

1 CORINTHIANS 13:4-7

Work at living in peace with everyone, and work at living a holy life, for those who are not holy will not see the Lord. Look after each other so that none of you fails to receive the grace of God. Watch out that no poisonous root of bitterness grows up to trouble you, corrupting many.

HEBREWS 12:14-15

Understand this, my dear brothers and sisters: You must all be quick to listen, slow to speak, and slow to get angry. Human anger does not produce the righteousness God desires.

JAMES 1:19-20

Words to Awaken Your Spirit

Forgiveness is unlocking the door to set someone free and realizing you were the prisoner!

MAX LUCADO

Forgiveness prompted by love is the only way to repair the devastation that so often mars our relationships.

DAVID JEREMIAH

Grace has to be the loveliest word in the English language. It embodies almost every attractive quality we hope to find in others. Grace is a gift of the humble to the humiliated. Grace acknowledges the ugliness of sin by choosing to see beyond it. Grace accepts a person as someone worthy of kindness despite whatever grime or hard-shell casing keeps him or her separated from the rest of the world. Grace is a gift of tender mercy when it makes the least sense.

CHARLES R. SWINDOLL

Forgiveness is not a feeling; it is a commitment. It is a choice to show mercy, not to hold the offense up against the offender. Forgiveness is an expression of love.

GARY CHAPMAN

To be a Christian means to forgive the inexcusable, because God has forgiven the inexcusable in you. This is hard. It is perhaps not so hard to forgive a single injury. But to forgive the incessant provocations of daily life—to keep on forgiving the bossy mother-in-law, the bullying husband, the nagging wife, the selfish daughter, the deceitful son—how can we do it? Only, I think, by remembering where we stand, by meaning our words when we say in our prayers each night, "Forgive us our trespasses as we forgive those who trespass against us." We are offered forgiveness on no other terms. To refuse it means to refuse God's mercy for ourselves. There is no hint of exceptions and God means what He says.

C. S. LEWIS

In the shadow of my hurt, forgiveness feels like a decision to reward my enemy. But in the shadow of the cross, forgiveness is merely a gift from one undeserving soul to another.

ANDY STANLEY

If Jesus forgave those who nailed Him to the cross, and if God forgives you and me, how can you withhold your forgiveness from someone else?

ANNE GRAHAM LOTZ

We are to forgive so that we may enjoy God's goodness without feeling the weight of anger burning deep within our hearts. Forgiveness does not mean we recant the fact that what happened to us was wrong. Instead, we roll our burdens onto the Lord and allow Him to carry them for us.

CHARLES STANLEY

Prayer for Hope and Healing

Lord, it can be so incredibly difficult to forgive someone who has hurt me. But I know that's exactly what you have called me to do. In fact, you forgive my sins and transgressions every day—all I have to do is ask. Lord, help me to get past the bitterness, anger, and resentment I am feeling so that I can forgive those who have hurt me. Help me show the same grace to others that you have shown to me—even if, like me, they may not be fully deserving of it. I don't want to waste one more moment of my life consumed by hatred and animosity.

In your Son's name, amen.

GUARD YOUR THOUGHTS

Nothing paralyzes our lives like the attitude that things can never change. We need to remind ourselves that God can change things! . . . Outlook determines outcome. If we see only the problems, we will be defeated; but if we see the possibilities in the problems, we can have victory.

WARREN WIERSBE

While there is certainly no shortage of pain and suffering in the world, sometimes the most toxic source of pain and stress can be found in our own heads. Ruminating on negative or painful experiences, refusing to forgive, or practicing a perennially negative outlook on life can create ongoing stress. What's more, because the source of this chronic stress isn't anything external that you can point to, it can be hard to identify and change. We all have an inner voice constantly blabbering about our faults, failures, inadequacies, and unfortunate experiences.

But you can control the on/off switch for that voice. Refuse to sit still for self-inflicted verbal beatings any longer, and dam the flow of negative messages coming into your brain. Replace them with positive truths. Accept your shortcomings and celebrate your strengths. Refuse to ruminate about past hurts and redirect your thoughts to uplifting memories. You are not a mere bystander in this battle. It's fully within your power to choose which thoughts and ideas you feed and which you starve. Nurture helpful, healing thoughts while banishing ones that bring you down and cause you doubt. Take a page from the apostle Paul:

Rejoice in the Lord always. I will say it again: Rejoice! Let your gentleness be evident to all. The Lord is near. Do not be anxious about anything, but in every situation, by prayer and petition, with thanksgiving, present your requests to God. And the peace of God, which transcends all understanding, will guard your hearts and your minds in Christ Jesus.

Finally, brothers and sisters, whatever is true, whatever is noble, whatever is right, whatever is pure, whatever is lovely,

whatever is admirable—if anything is
excellent or praiseworthy— think about
such things.

PHILIPPIANS 4:4-8, NIV

Remember, while negative emotions can sap us of our mental and physical strength, the opposite is also true: positive emotions invigorate us, giving us the boost we need to continue through difficult stretches. Make guarding your thoughts a regular habit. Be intentional about identifying the thoughts that are dragging you down and replacing them with thoughts that lift you up. Your soul will thank you for it.

Scripture to Soothe Your Soul

Set your minds on things that are above, not on
things that are on earth.

COLOSSIANS 3:2, ESV

Look straight ahead,
    and fix your eyes on what lies before you.

PROVERBS 4:25

Seek the Kingdom of God above all else, and
live righteously, and he will give you everything
you need.

MATTHEW 6:33

Oh, the joys of those who do not
    follow the advice of the wicked,
    or stand around with sinners,
    or join in with mockers.
But they delight in the law of the LORD,
    meditating on it day and night.
They are like trees planted along the
        riverbank,
    bearing fruit each season.
Their leaves never wither,
    and they prosper in all they do.

But not the wicked!
    They are like worthless chaff, scattered by the
        wind.
They will be condemned at the time of
        judgment.
    Sinners will have no place among the godly.

For the LORD watches over the path of the
    godly,
  but the path of the wicked leads to destruction.
PSALM 1

The temptations in your life are no different from
what others experience. And God is faithful. He
will not allow the temptation to be more than
you can stand. When you are tempted, he will
show you a way out so that you can endure.
1 CORINTHIANS 10:13

Since we are surrounded by such a huge crowd
of witnesses to the life of faith, let us strip off
every weight that slows us down, especially the
sin that so easily trips us up. And let us run with
endurance the race God has set before us. We do
this by keeping our eyes on Jesus, the champion
who initiates and perfects our faith. Because
of the joy awaiting him, he endured the cross,
disregarding its shame. Now he is seated in the
place of honor beside God's throne.
HEBREWS 12:1-2

Put away all malice and all deceit and hypocrisy and envy and all slander. Like newborn infants, long for the pure spiritual milk, that by it you may grow up into salvation.

1 PETER 2:1-2, ESV

Don't copy the behavior and customs of this world, but let God transform you into a new person by changing the way you think. Then you will learn to know God's will for you, which is good and pleasing and perfect.

ROMANS 12:2

Seek his will in all you do,
    and he will show you which path to take.

PROVERBS 3:6

Words to Awaken Your Spirit

[Spiritual strongholds] begin with a thought. One thought becomes a consideration.

A consideration develops into an attitude,
which leads them to action. Action repeated
becomes a habit, and a habit establishes
a "power base for the enemy," that is, a
stronghold.

ELISABETH ELLIOT

I am a spiritual being. After this body is dead,
my spirit will soar. I refuse to let what will rot,
rule the eternal. I choose self-control. I will be
drunk only by joy. I will be impassioned only
by my faith. I will be influenced only by God.
I will be taught only by Christ.

MAX LUCADO

I can't control the things that happen to me
each day, but I can control how I think about
them. I can say to myself, "I have a choice
to have destructive thoughts or constructive
thoughts right now. I can wallow in what's
wrong and make things worse, or I can ask God
for a better perspective to help me see good
even when I don't feel good." Indeed, when we

gain new perspectives, we can see new ways of thinking.

LYSA TERKEURST

The longer I live, the more convinced I become that life is 10 percent what happens to you and 90 percent how we respond to it. . . . I believe the single most significant decision I can make on a day-to-day basis is my choice of attitude. It is more important than my past, my education, my bankroll, my successes or failures, fame or pain, what other people think of me or say about me, my circumstances, or my position.

CHARLES R. SWINDOLL

God is never a God of discouragement. When you have a discouraging spirit or train of thought in your mind, you can be sure it is not from God. He sometimes brings pain to his children—conviction over sin, or repentance over fallenness, or challenges that scare us, or visions of his holiness that overwhelm us. But God never brings discouragement.

JOHN ORTBERG

Every human activity, except sin, can be done for God's pleasure if you do it with an attitude of praise.

RICK WARREN

Many things are possible for the person who has hope. Even more is possible for the person who has faith. And still more is possible for the person who knows how to love. But everything is possible for the person who practices all three virtues.

BROTHER LAWRENCE

The way to be truly happy is by being truly human, and the way to be truly human is to be truly godly.

J. I. PACKER

Pray, and let God worry.

MARTIN LUTHER

Courage doesn't mean we're not afraid anymore, it just means our actions aren't controlled by our doubts.

BOB GOFF

Prayer for Hope and Healing

God, it is amazing to me how much my mind can wander in the course of a single day. If I'm not careful, petty annoyances, unspoken frustrations, and perceived injustices can occupy my every waking thought. I might not be able to control what is happening around me every day, but I can control the way I respond and react to it. You have advised us to "fix [our] thoughts on what is true, and honorable, and right, and pure, and lovely, and admirable, [and to] think [only] about things that are excellent and worthy of praise." Lord, don't let me become mired in the negative, but rather help me to keep my heart and mind focused on you and on all of the wonderful blessings you have bestowed upon me, because that is where true happiness lies.

It is in your name I pray, amen.

LAUGHTER

Laughter is the most beautiful and beneficial
therapy God ever granted humanity.

CHARLES R. SWINDOLL

Sometimes wisdom can be found in the most unlikely places. That's certainly true of this lyric from a 1977 hit song by Jimmy Buffett: "If we couldn't laugh, we would all go insane." Now, I doubt Buffett knew at the time that he had science on his side, but as it turns out, the physical, psychological, and emotional payoff of laughter is no joke. In fact, studies have shown that laughter is good for your health. Among the benefits identified by recent studies are

- reduced stress levels,
- improved immune system function,

- increased levels of endorphins, the body's natural painkillers, and
- increased heart rate and oxygenation of vital organs.[5]

See? Laughter really *is* the best medicine! It's also good for your soul. Contrary to what many people might think, God does want us to be happy. Why else would he have given us the gift of humor, levity, and wit? As Christian author Jennifer Dukes Lee writes, "The devil didn't make art, laughter, music, or Sunday afternoon naps. God did!"[6] Even David, after emerging from a season of sorrow, wrote, "You have turned my mourning into joyful dancing. You have taken away my clothes of mourning and clothed me with joy, that I might sing praises to you and not be silent" (Psalm 30:11-12).

Accessing our God-given lightheartedness is a surefire way to combat sorrow and despair. If you make a conscious effort to find the humor in the everyday and keep your ears and eyes tuned in to the lighter side of life, I bet you'll find that the laughter you've been missing lately was right there inside you all along.

Scripture to Soothe Your Soul

For everything there is a season,
    a time for every activity under heaven. . . .
A time to cry and a time to laugh.
    A time to grieve and a time to dance.

ECCLESIASTES 3:1, 4

Blessed are you who are hungry now,
    for you shall be satisfied.
Blessed are you who weep now,
    for you shall laugh.

LUKE 6:21, ESV

Rejoice in the LORD and be glad, all you who obey
        him!
    Shout for joy, all you whose hearts are pure!

PSALM 32:11

I [Paul] pray that God, the source of hope, will fill
you completely with joy and peace because you
trust in him. Then you will overflow with confident
hope through the power of the Holy Spirit.

ROMANS 15:13

Delight yourself in the Lord,
    and he will give you the desires of your heart.

PSALM 37:4, ESV

A glad heart makes a happy face;
    a broken heart crushes the spirit.

PROVERBS 15:13

His anger lasts only a moment,
    but his favor lasts a lifetime!
Weeping may last through the night,
    but joy comes with the morning.

PSALM 30:5

I decided there is nothing better than to enjoy
food and drink and to find satisfaction in work.
Then I realized that these pleasures are from the
hand of God.

ECCLESIASTES 2:24

You will show me the way of life,
    granting me the joy of your presence
    and the pleasures of living with you forever.

PSALM 16:11

Wisdom to Awaken Your Spirit

Good humor and laughter are far too
wonderful not to come straight from the heart
of God.

BETH MOORE

Good-humor makes all things tolerable.

HENRY WARD BEECHER

Joy, not grit, is the hallmark of holy obedience.
We need to be light-hearted in what we do
to avoid taking ourselves too seriously. It is a
cheerful revolt against self and pride.

RICHARD J. FOSTER

I cannot even imagine where I would be today
were it not for that handful of friends who have
given me a heart full of joy. Let's face it, friends
make life a lot more fun.

CHARLES R. SWINDOLL

Joy is really the simplest form of gratitude.

KARL BARTH

Joy is the serious business of Heaven.

C. S. LEWIS

If you have no joy in your religion, there's a leak
in your Christianity somewhere.

BILLY SUNDAY

It is not how much we have, but how much we
enjoy, that makes happiness.

CHARLES SPURGEON

Our inner desire for happiness isn't a sin. It's a
desire planted in us by God himself.

JENNIFER DUKES LEE

Man is more himself, man is more manlike,
when joy is the fundamental thing in him,
and grief the superficial. Melancholy should
be an innocent interlude, a tender and fugitive
frame of mind; praise should be the permanent
pulsation of the soul. Pessimism is at best an
emotional half-holiday; joy is the uproarious
labour by which all things live.

G. K. CHESTERTON

Prayer for Hope and Healing

Father God, sometimes the challenges and difficulties of everyday life can become so overwhelming that it's easy for me to lose sight of all the good that exists in the world. And yet there is so much that is good in this world. Art, music, nature, great food, friendship—you created all of these things. In fact, "every good and perfect gift" comes from you. Thank you, God, for the gifts of joy and love and laughter. These are the things that make life worth living. These are the things that bring light into the darkness. And these are the things that remind me, in my darkest hours, that the best is yet to come.

In Jesus' name I pray, amen.

PART 2

Verses to Mend Your Soul

WHEN YOU'RE FEELING HOPELESS

"I know the plans I have for you," says the
LORD. "They are plans for good and not for
disaster, to give you a future and a hope."
JEREMIAH 29:11

May the God of hope fill you with all joy and
peace in believing, so that by the power of the
Holy Spirit you may abound in hope.
ROMANS 15:13, ESV

Rejoice in our confident hope. Be patient in
trouble, and keep on praying.
ROMANS 12:12

Those who trust in the LORD will find new strength.
They will soar high on wings like eagles.

They will run and not grow weary.
　　They will walk and not faint.
ISAIAH 40:31

Be strong and courageous! Do not be afraid and
do not panic before them. For the LORD your
God will personally go ahead of you. He will
neither fail you nor abandon you.
DEUTERONOMY 31:6

The LORD hears his people when they call to him
　　for help.
　　He rescues them from all their troubles.
The LORD is close to the brokenhearted;
　　he rescues those whose spirits are crushed.

The righteous person faces many troubles,
　　but the LORD comes to the rescue each time.
For the LORD protects the bones of the righteous;
　　not one of them is broken!
PSALM 34:17-20

Come to me [Jesus], all of you who are weary
and carry heavy burdens, and I will give you

rest. Take my yoke upon you. Let me teach you,
because I am humble and gentle at heart, and
you will find rest for your souls. For my yoke is
easy to bear, and the burden I give you is light.
MATTHEW 11:28-30

Surely your goodness and unfailing love will
        pursue me
    all the days of my life,
and I will live in the house of the LORD forever.
PSALM 23:6

For God so loved the world that he gave his
one and only Son, that whoever believes in him
shall not perish but have eternal life.
JOHN 3:16, NIV

Because of our faith, Christ has brought us into
this place of undeserved privilege where we now
stand, and we confidently and joyfully look
forward to sharing God's glory. We can rejoice,
too, when we run into problems and trials, for
we know that they help us develop endurance.
And endurance develops strength of character,

and character strengthens our confident hope of salvation. And this hope will not lead to disappointment. For we know how dearly God loves us, because he has given us the Holy Spirit to fill our hearts with his love.

ROMANS 5:2-5

WHEN YOU'RE FEELING ANXIOUS

Worry weighs a person down;
    an encouraging word cheers a person up.
PROVERBS 12:25

Don't worry about anything; instead, pray
about everything. Tell God what you need, and
thank him for all he has done. Then you will
experience God's peace, which exceeds anything
we can understand. His peace will guard your
hearts and minds as you live in Christ Jesus.
PHILIPPIANS 4:6-7

That is why I [Jesus] tell you not to worry
about everyday life—whether you have enough
food and drink, or enough clothes to wear. Isn't
life more than food, and your body more than

clothing? Look at the birds. They don't plant or harvest or store food in barns, for your heavenly Father feeds them. And aren't you far more valuable to him than they are? Can all your worries add a single moment to your life?

And why worry about your clothing? Look at the lilies of the field and how they grow. They don't work or make their clothing, yet Solomon in all his glory was not dressed as beautifully as they are. And if God cares so wonderfully for wildflowers that are here today and thrown into the fire tomorrow, he will certainly care for you. Why do you have so little faith?

So don't worry about these things, saying, "What will we eat? What will we drink? What will we wear?" These things dominate the thoughts of unbelievers, but your heavenly Father already knows all your needs. Seek the Kingdom of God above all else, and live righteously, and he will give you everything you need.

So don't worry about tomorrow, for tomorrow will bring its own worries. Today's trouble is enough for today.

MATTHEW 6:25-34

I can do everything through Christ, who gives
me strength.

PHILIPPIANS 4:13

We can say with confidence,

"The Lord is my helper,
    so I will have no fear.
    What can mere people do to me?"

HEBREWS 13:6

This is my [the Lord's] command—be
strong and courageous! Do not be afraid or
discouraged. For the Lord your God is with
you wherever you go.

JOSHUA 1:9

I [Jesus] am leaving you with a gift—peace of
mind and heart. And the peace I give is a gift the
world cannot give. So don't be troubled or afraid.

JOHN 14:27

Don't let your hearts be troubled. Trust in God,
and trust also in me [Jesus]. There is more than

enough room in my Father's home. If this were not so, would I have told you that I am going to prepare a place for you? When everything is ready, I will come and get you, so that you will always be with me where I am. And you know the way to where I am going.

JOHN 14:1-4

God has not given us a spirit of fear and timidity, but of power, love, and self-discipline.

2 TIMOTHY 1:7

Give your burdens to the LORD,
    and he will take care of you.
    He will not permit the godly to slip and fall.

PSALM 55:22

WHEN YOU NEED ENCOURAGEMENT

Trust in the Lord with all your heart;
    do not depend on your own understanding.
Seek his will in all you do,
    and he will show you which path to take.

PROVERBS 3:5-6

This is my [the Lord's] command—be
strong and courageous! Do not be afraid or
discouraged. For the Lord your God is with
you wherever you go.

JOSHUA 1:9

What shall we say about such wonderful things
as these? If God is for us, who can ever be
against us?

ROMANS 8:31

I [Paul] pray that God, the source of hope, will fill you completely with joy and peace because you trust in him. Then you will overflow with confident hope through the power of the Holy Spirit.

ROMANS 15:13

My dear brothers and sisters, be strong and immovable. Always work enthusiastically for the Lord, for you know that nothing you do for the Lord is ever useless.

1 CORINTHIANS 15:58

Be strong and courageous,
    all you who put your hope in the LORD!

PSALM 31:24

Do not be afraid or discouraged, for the LORD will personally go ahead of you. He will be with you; he will neither fail you nor abandon you.

DEUTERONOMY 31:8

Don't be afraid, for I am with you.
    Don't be discouraged, for I am your God.

I will strengthen you and help you.
  I will hold you up with my victorious right
    hand.

See, all your angry enemies lie there,
  confused and humiliated.
Anyone who opposes you will die
  and come to nothing.
You will look in vain
  for those who tried to conquer you.
Those who attack you
  will come to nothing.
For I hold you by your right hand—
  I, the LORD your God.
And I say to you,
  "Don't be afraid. I am here to help you.
Though you are a lowly worm, O Jacob,
  don't be afraid, people of Israel, for I will help you.
I am the LORD, your Redeemer.
  I am the Holy One of Israel."

ISAIAH 41:10-14

Blessed are the poor in spirit,
  for theirs is the kingdom of heaven.

Blessed are those who mourn,
> for they will be comforted.

Blessed are the meek,
> for they will inherit the earth.

Blessed are those who hunger and thirst for
> righteousness,
> for they will be filled.

Blessed are the merciful,
> for they will be shown mercy.

Blessed are the pure in heart,
> for they will see God.

Blessed are the peacemakers,
> for they will be called children of God.

Blessed are those who are persecuted because of
> righteousness,
> for theirs is the kingdom of heaven.

Blessed are you when people insult you, persecute you and falsely say all kinds of evil against you because of me [Jesus]. Rejoice and be glad, because great is your reward in heaven, for in the same way they persecuted the prophets who were before you.

MATTHEW 5:3-12, NIV

WHEN YOU ARE EXHAUSTED

Don't be afraid, for I am with you.
Don't be discouraged, for I am your God.
I will strengthen you and help you.
I will hold you up with my victorious right
hand.

ISAIAH 41:10

Those who trust in the LORD will find new
strength.
They will soar high on wings like eagles.
They will run and not grow weary.
They will walk and not faint.

ISAIAH 40:31

The temptations in your life are no different
from what others experience. And God is

faithful. He will not allow the temptation to be more than you can stand. When you are tempted, he will show you a way out so that you can endure.

1 CORINTHIANS 10:13

The LORD is my strength and my song;
    he has given me victory.
This is my God, and I will praise him—
    my father's God, and I will exalt him!

EXODUS 15:2

A final word: Be strong in the Lord and in his mighty power.

EPHESIANS 6:10

The LORD your God is going with you! He will fight for you against your enemies, and he will give you victory!

DEUTERONOMY 20:4

Each time he [the Lord] said, "My grace is all you need. My power works best in weakness." So now I [Paul] am glad to boast about my

weaknesses, so that the power of Christ
can work through me. That's why I take
pleasure in my weaknesses, and in the insults,
hardships, persecutions, and troubles that
I suffer for Christ. For when I am weak, then
I am strong.

2 CORINTHIANS 12:9-10

The Holy Spirit helps us in our weakness. For
example, we don't know what God wants us
to pray for. But the Holy Spirit prays for us
with groanings that cannot be expressed in
words. And the Father who knows all hearts
knows what the Spirit is saying, for the Spirit
pleads for us believers in harmony with God's
own will.

ROMANS 8:26-27

You will receive power when the Holy
Spirit comes upon you. And you will be my
[Jesus'] witnesses, telling people about me
everywhere—in Jerusalem, throughout Judea,
in Samaria, and to the ends of the earth.

ACTS 1:8

WHEN YOU
LACK FOCUS

Commit your actions to the LORD,
  and your plans will succeed.

PROVERBS 16:3

I [Paul] don't mean to say that I have already
achieved these things or that I have already
reached perfection. But I press on to possess
that perfection for which Christ Jesus first
possessed me. No, dear brothers and sisters,
I have not achieved it, but I focus on this
one thing: Forgetting the past and looking
forward to what lies ahead, I press on to reach
the end of the race and receive the heavenly
prize for which God, through Christ Jesus, is
calling us.

PHILIPPIANS 3:12-14

The one who endures to the end will be saved.
MATTHEW 24:13

Since we are surrounded by such a huge crowd
of witnesses to the life of faith, let us strip off
every weight that slows us down, especially the
sin that so easily trips us up. And let us run
with endurance the race God has set before us.
We do this by keeping our eyes on Jesus, the
champion who initiates and perfects our faith.
Because of the joy awaiting him, he endured
the cross, disregarding its shame. Now he
is seated in the place of honor beside God's
throne.

HEBREWS 12:1-2

You can enter God's Kingdom only through
the narrow gate. The highway to hell is broad,
and its gate is wide for the many who choose
that way. But the gateway to life is very narrow
and the road is difficult, and only a few ever
find it.

MATTHEW 7:13-14

My child, never forget the things I have taught you.
     Store my commands in your heart.
If you do this, you will live many years,
     and your life will be satisfying.
Never let loyalty and kindness leave you!
     Tie them around your neck as a reminder.
     Write them deep within your heart.
Then you will find favor with both God and people,
     and you will earn a good reputation.

Trust in the LORD with all your heart;
     do not depend on your own understanding.
Seek his will in all you do,
     and he will show you which path to take.
PROVERBS 3:1-6

Seek the Kingdom of God above all else, and
live righteously, and he will give you everything
you need.
MATTHEW 6:33

Think about the things of heaven, not the
things of earth.
COLOSSIANS 3:2

Study this Book of Instruction continually.
Meditate on it day and night so you will be sure
to obey everything written in it. Only then will
you prosper and succeed in all you do.

JOSHUA 1:8

Notes

1. Charles R. Swindoll, *Hope Again* (Nashville: Thomas Nelson, 1996), 277.
2. Elisabeth Elliot, *Let Me Be a Woman* (Carol Stream, IL: Tyndale, 2013), 9.
3. Corporation for National and Community Service, *The Health Benefits of Volunteering*, April 2007, https://www.nationalservice.gov/pdf/07_0506_hbr.pdf.
4. Frederick Buechner, *Beyond Words: Daily Readings in the ABC's of Faith* (New York: HarperCollins, 2004), 18.
5. "Stress Relief from Laughter? It's No Joke," Mayo Clinic, April 21, 2016, https://www.mayoclinic.org/healthy-lifestyle/stress-management/in-depth/stress-relief/art-20044456.
6. Jennifer Dukes Lee, *The Happiness Dare: Pursuing Your Heart's Deepest, Holiest, and Most Vulnerable Desire* (Carol Stream, IL: Tyndale, 2016), 68.

About the Authors

Dr. Gregory Jantz is a trusted and highly sought-after mental health expert, speaker, and bestselling author. Dr. Jantz is known for developing whole-person care of depression, anxiety, eating disorders, and PTSD, and he founded The Center: A Place of Hope, which has been voted one of the top ten facilities in the United States for the treatment of depression. Dr. Jantz has appeared on NBC, CNN, FOX, ABC, and CBS; has been interviewed for the *New York Post*, Associated Press, *Family Circle*, *Woman's Day*, Yahoo .com, MSNBC.com; and is a regular contributor to *Huffington Post* and *Psychology Today*. Dr. Jantz is the bestselling author of thirty-five books, including *Gotta Have It!: Freedom from Wanting Everything Right*

Here, Right Now; Healing the Scars of Emotional Abuse; and *The Stranger in Your House.* He has been married thirty-five years to his wife, LaFon, and is the father of two sons, Gregg and Benjamin.

Keith Wall, a twenty-five-year publishing veteran, is an award-winning author, magazine editor, radio script-writer, and online columnist. He currently writes full time in collaboration with several bestselling authors. Keith lives in a mountaintop cabin near Manitou Springs, Colorado.

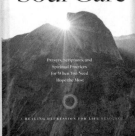